TRE PAESı

&

OTHER POEMS

TRE PAESI *&* OTHER POEMS

Peter Makin

ISOBAR
PRESS

First published in 2023 by

Isobar Press
Sakura 2-21-23-202, Setagaya-ku,
Tokyo 156-0053, Japan

&

14 Isokon Flats, Lawn Road,
London NW3 2XD, United Kingdom

https://isobarpress.com

ISBN 978-4-907359-42-3

Cover and author photos by Peter Makin.

CONTENTS

TRE PAESI

OTHER POEMS

TRE PAESI

North Kyoto

the silver sea
              of cloud
fills up between ridges
leaks over the edge

the shell of ice
from the splashes thrown up by the fall
peels off the sides of a leaf
split down its back

tiny contributive stream adding its heartbeat
to the small torrent

              looping from hollow to hollow
              & afterwards blankness
                        'the vale of the years'
              down that dark path towards nobody.

In the morning my dreams come to me acutely
and painfully; in the evening
elegiacally

Swooping down over an endless series of textures
golden-grained, glassy,
flat water, beach,
paths of ragged cracked rocks
cut through rocks
which I needn't touch
because I was flying, calling
'Correa' at every interval, lest she be out of sight
                                        among rocks
holding Pending

To betray the thought into words
still having meaning.

Cicada's wing, inching its way across the concrete
under the propulsion of 5 ants.

After the storm
swept and laid
but not orderly
the wet clumps at all angles,
waiting for the hand of the labourer
to grip it
        by the base, and cut;
smoke-odour from the far side of the valley
& the million crickets'
sounds
        in layers,
background, then foreground,
invisible. Another
autumn

searching the signs in my heart
my lying heart:
sawdust, ashes, falsity, misery,
panic.
You could toss a coin and which would you go with,
the fear?
All I want to do is to sit down for ten minutes
& stare at the wind

grassblades always uncatching,
unbending themselves from
the weight of a grasshopper
or a frog that's jumped

ripples of bark like a cow's hide
round a prong half-surfacing
two ants meet & nuzzle
on the slope of the limb half-way up

you have to be tough to live a non-life like mine.
At least learned Japanese? No? Can't speak it?
at least learned the words for ...
trimming-shears 刈込鋏.

I have earned my exile.

where the water curls over like lumpen glass

take to the stream and
leave no tracks
up the gully
where no voice is
only the river, breaking stones
and the fingers of old bamboo
bearing snow.

The eyesight shrinking back, like an old turtle

and then comes the taptap of the woodpecker
and he says: Cease from
striving.

The leaves
are silent, with the light on them,

and he said: Cease
your striving.

I look around for more,
to make a moment of this,
and he's gone.

Cease from
striving.

The soft rhythm of the sifting
                                    of the small beans
by the old pair, kneeling in the yard next door
with dulling sunlight at an earlier
hour of the day,
            persimmons lonelier
on their trees, as their leaves grow richer
in lustrous
green, red and brown, in a continuum of quiet, with
        that slight rounding of the membrane
                                    between the veins
as they turn colour

The lion-dogs with their curly manes
and pearly teeth
in fresh grey granite.

now then, husk of a [   ], clinging tightly to a
                        [   ],
I expect you've been gone over by the local ants,
                    who found
nothing but the
    forma and 形 *katachi* of a once-noisy [   ].
Plato would have liked that pure immaterial [   ].

an intimate knowledge of tree-barks
and of the way a pee-line cuts back through
the snow towards one's boots,
failing.

The great creeper that
grows and strangles
and brings down a tree
lies wrapped around its companion
in the morning wood.

Lie tight to the earth
hear that tiny crinkling, which
is not only of the leaves you are stirring
but of the very light snowfall
now falling on them.

Beatrice is a lay figure (says Coleridge), by which he means a
plaster cutout, someone the poet energetically
repents to, about whom he remembers
nothing. I found a pen up here of some weeks ago
mute evidence of my lucubrations,
of which fruit there is none
except phrases like this

My mind is a ferment of old desires
(with the rain-drops on the back of my neck)
to build Vesuvius or defend Thermopylae.
but if I can no longer
make out the glisten on the tree-trunks

Whenever a song breaks
particularly forth,
it is that you are crowding out
a thought you don't want.

An airliner, striving across from the moon to Venus
partly occluded by a cloud
with its lights blinking bravely
rice-fields
abandoned to unthinned cedars, which are
starving each other of space

The water is beginning to flood
        creepingly the furrows of the rice-fields,
the *kek-*
kyoku bird marking its sound-curls
in the evening air;
noise of remote airliner
remotely from over the hill's edge.
Slowly the water percolates,
osmoses, loosens earth into mud,
renews;
        the sky darkening,
time to loosen the limbs
and go home.

14

Autumn reflected in the grey-green water,
the tree already past its full yellow,
outer branches bare,
                    leaves
one by one
waveringly
to earth.
What promises what hopes what repetitions
under these
siftings, while the metacycle
moves to its close.

your spiderweb
revealed to all the world by the mist-drops, Mr Spider:
thwarted again.

An analogous mind:
He see the pipe
disconnected, with the clear column
from the one end pouring futilely
over the back of the other,
he think of his life

Tailoring bits of reality
reassembled, trimmed

The bird that is trying to pass itself off as an iron door
weakened with rust
        with bars over a small window,
and a different sound on its opening
from its closing again;

the calm voice of the toad
uninfluenced by my bear-bell;

                              and,

bloating and debloating
like a slack frog
              in the sunlight,
a rough stone
with the intermittent waves welling over it.
Made sure of it by touching.

put my head into a whole caul of spiderweb
and clawed it off, swearing

The lurid tower is only light, a
ragged gap caught in the clouds:
the dark fluff stacked up all around
                              this valley.
Crickets industriously chirm,
water flows. Damp
and reproduction and death
which will all be slowed down
                              only a little
by the arrival of winter.

The clouds are just clearing the mountains,
always urgent to make it east
before night

Une eau très claire
and I drink at the swell of it.

little pillars of mud, each
protected by its one small rock
                    from the rain.

Does it give you a sense of power,
                    Mr Spider,
twelve feet from the ground, four feet
        from any outstretched bough,
sitting in mid-nothing,
waiting?

Small beer
        to the buzzard
hanging between mountains

Cumbria

the ripples make Gothic peaks
                    where they join
in the stiff breeze

seen from the cavern of the back of my hood
that the wind beats sideways,
the mist passes in rags
and from time to time Winton Fell
                appears to my left
under a pearly sun and is gone again.

They say you can see Solway Firth from here,
                glinting
sounds of the sheep bleating,
lapwings
      crying

Rabbit skidded
on exit from burrow to cinders, seeing me,
and I am being eaten by horseflies.
I will seat myself on this bole
            in the sunny shade, to note this
        and be further eaten.
           Old sloe-trees,
well rooted into the slag
      that made the railway,
with the rabbits' unknown cities
      now underneath
where they pause, just for a moment,
           in front of their portals
and (whoops!) they are gone.

This slope was near to the limit of what a locomotive
                                        could handle
in those days.
            Cold Keld filled with 40 navvies there to build it.
The stump of a cast-iron
            cruciform railway-level
            signpost, cracked off, polished by sheep
rubbing their itches, leaving their sheepgrease
round the bright part,
a good angle and height to scratch against.

Meet the flat rabbit corpse
                        caked with fur.
The lamb stops to sniff the branch I have handled.
A little nervosity in the words ... is a good thing.
And how would you imitate their sound?
BLEUGHGHGHGH ...

The sheep's back's shudders, back and forth,
that ripple along the body
            breathing heat.

The philosophical stone flags
have ripples in them like
                        cast lead
under the edge of the sun
            that comes in under the bog door
to where they break
with light mud-dust over them

Two or three
trembling leaves
making a tapping sound
in the evening breeze
                as the sun goes down.
With many a dark incantation
from behind his deaf ear

which should have been a good, complete,
                                powerful painting
and wasn't; they won't know she just
ran out of steam,
        or why.
                In a marine blue plastic-shiny coat
with red edgings
on a rice-field, cut into a steep slope,
after harvest, out in the sun:
legs apart to balance her on the painting-stool,
open-angled brush-arm,
body,
        parasol,
                painting-stool, opened
        as if all of her were an open parasol
focussed down-valley; with a great hat
as if everything were opening up
around the line of her gaze
downwind

and my miserable exit from Lincoln on
                        the National Bus
all full of lies and plans

said Atul Shah: 'she is at a turning-point'

'How're ye gettin' on wi' your
                wife, Mr Makin?' said
Dr Latto

put your phone on a dried
                          sheep-crud
and wait for the message to go.

Ô small peace
with the sun warming through the jeans on the inner leg
and the smooth cracked limbs of fallen bush
the rowan still more orange than red
and the moss just holding its own against the
                continuing drought
and the single buzzard crying.

Teesdale fells past the remaining abutment
                                    of the bridge
and for a moment I thought they were
                moving with the cloud-bank.

Tiny scapula among the cinders
next to the sheep-crud:
the cinders that came here by the waggon-load
along the railway half-built
to build it out further.
A signal-box entirely filled by an alder
climbing to the light, over the floor-
                timbers fallen in a maze.

eaten by other worlds
other regrets

These lichen-patches, their
mosaic, grey, grey-green, so
perfectly fitting, the borders
must be the battle-lines
where their colonies meet?
20 years' stasis,
glacial war.

How many generations of rabbits
since she painted here?
cropping the grass
            sharp-toothed
        under the birches bent by the same wind
which she steadied herself against with her easel:
while the birches turned into
grass; the
        rabbits into mangled fur
and sod; and the birch-trunks
              still weaving
in the dance in which she then
painted them.

and wouldn't it be
that the solidest remnant of all this skill
    and labour, the
thousands of tons of spent cinder
        waggoned in from Darlington,
formed to make a curve
                coming

out of the cutting
            you could
        see from the moon
is now rabbit-home:
galleried and interconnected
rabbit-home,
wormed and tunneled like old cowshit,
under a crust likewise thin

Barrelling back to their mother
            for her teats,
with their tails wiggling like idiots
            as they suckle in,
from which she breaks off
to investigate me

the pleasure of distance
you watch those trees heave
like a storm at sea,

the pipey, gurgling
            cry of the snipe
rising,
gliding back
            down again

Lincolnshire

Fearing my hat had fallen off my
handlebars but it was on my
head. My head still
where it had been,
to judge from the position of my hat,
which was not on my handlebars.

Encircled by the ocean of
          the sound of the people on their
          way to work,
downhill into the wind,
uphill with it behind you,
Fulnetby over there somewhere in the trees,
the larks belting it away
and the cold wind carrying the stink of the chicken-farm
away from you;

lichen on the hedges bright, almost
                              yellow-green
waiting to be hidden by leaves,
and the sound-ocean.

the moorhen's feet in
          the reverse direction of each other
as I thought, in the soft mud
like any new leaf unfurled.

always embarrassed, embarrassing,
          ill at ease
and alone,
evenings bored

and taking walks, and sitting
        on a piece of cold concrete
watching in a stupor a piece of
        catkin dancing on the
        end of a spiderline

make myself sit here till the sun's gone.

Mr Myxomatosis
Rabbit, with
shrunken skull and fat eyes
you are your own universe, all hell,
and nothing to wait for.

Curled over in grief
blasted by the weedspray
backs of the nettles raised to the wind;
thumb of the old water-tower
and everywhere the young swallows
        chirbling urgently
as if the world depended on their urgency

things lived
        and relived
lose themselves in nothingness

I align an oak, far off in the mist,
up from the left of which leads
a hedge

by where we set off to walk up
along the woods
    in the mist behind
with a dip in the trees, nearer
and less misty,
and down the centre of oak and dip, thus aligned,
  think I find
meaning.

The crinkly leaves of the brambles
      so young
wet with dew

Where there are barley-heads, lost from the last crop
  growing over the wheat, a
fluff of light green

Shimmering, blowing nettles
in the lowering sun
each one transparenter than the one
      behind it
except where the shadow of the one makes part of
the other opaque.

Take temporary shelter behind a
    clump of trees
beside a pond, and dislodge
a moorhen taking temporary shelter
in the pond;
the ripples overtake larger ripples,
  sideways, hither and thither;
the left eye waters with the wind.

New nettles coming up between the
        old stalks:
return of the seasons, which have no end,
though they will have end
for me and the waterhen.

The arid cap upended
on the table by the bottle with the
pale blue water
and the dead pizza.
Tant de culture, tant de vie vécue
and in the end we sink,
grabbing at lines of thought lost, like
                lost DNA:
fossilized reproduction, in plastic, of
        a mound of spaghetti, tacked on the wall
                in a restaurant in the Alto Adige, faithfully
coloured with Parmesan.

That everything takes you back
        to things undone
projects unfinished
angels with six wings
                        in the plastic drawer labelled
        ??
and probably still so labelled
in the empty farmhouse

All brown were the leaves
and fallen
crinkledly on the forest floor,
winding down towards Montaperti,
when she last painted.

Still know the density of that wood, in that photo,
how my thumb-nail
would go into it, but not my
thumb, as far as the soft part,
on the *shōji* behind her
and she, whose hair I could now brush aside
and kiss, as to her forehead
           (olive oil)
she with strange fingers
           bent a little back,
with a little gloss from over-wear
           on her padded Chinese jacket:
only a woman,
holding a cat, scratching its belly,
while the cat gazes up at her in daft ecstasy.

The endless parabolas of the swallows
in search of insects
           one foot above the ocean of white barley.

Butterflies cavorting in white
on a rich grey horizon;
barley shimmering in heat;
willow-leaves silver

Embalming in my verbal
spittle the
        brave gestures of my dead wife:
the steady movements of the paper-wasp's jaws at his
paper-nest-building

Climber tendrils
tangling with each other in the air, each
using the other to
climb free

old beet-leaf eaten
by bugs, half-yellow,
        in a field of mud, within sight of
Collow,
wave in the wind: you
can't help but return to the position
you first thought of;
        have no choice, with the
cellulose
        in your cells, and
the lull in the wind:
        back to square one. Wave in the wind.

The ball in the weir, the toy at the foot of the stair,
                                                falling over,
re-climbing:
Fuchū, 40 years gone

Except that now I no longer think
        some woman will rescue me,
some female with appealing eyes,

she being part of the cellulose, or of the wind.

There where
one of those molecules
shall go, from the wet rut, in the field,
into the land-drain,
others shall follow.
Making a little stream
or rivulet,
and then
a river. This is called history,
or fact. Good morning, Mr History,
the wind's behind you.

And in conclusion

陳 CHIN, to state, relate; get warped; old grain, old goods;
                                                        precocity

Lock into place
        (Easter Monday)
the lower wood
        and the upper wood,
lit up by rape
        glowing yellow,
sloping up
        to where the angles meet;
a few sheep browse at your crotch

At sixty, my ear was an obedient organ *for the reception of truth.*
                                                        Anal. 2.4.

That it is universal, is evident
as the grass grows out of the bark
                        of the fallen branch,
as the broken cow-parsley smells of
                                broken cow-
parsley,
as the small train goes on its way
                                        at 8.17

妖 Yō, attractive, bewitching; calamity

now I am in amaze how I transcend these lightsome bodies
                                        Par. 1.98-9

and Jerome has turned up, not
without his rock.

'You think you don't need me now. You needed me
                                        in Hiroshima.'

All time must terminate:
it is now,
        and it isn't
                and an instant will determine;
a moment, and it (I)
        will be over

Soft furry barley
bowing your heads, splaying out your spikes
and suddenly you're wheat
stubborn and ragged and stubby
the rabbits break your outliers
        and strip your heads
and strew them *par terre,*
speckled with mud

'We have wasted so much time'

Justified by some inner truth,
some higher value,
some hoped-for poethood.

Charles Vernon could see I was
writing more than I knew (so
could Peter Goldsbury).

'Never mind the quality'

And me to him: *Must needs be an effluence*
from the blessed movers   *Par.* 2.129

my pen paused on its way
        back into the cap, like
your dead match, always, on its way
        back into the box
– is this the right place to put it?
– it always was
in your long thin slightly
curved-back
fingers

陳 *hine*, old grain; old goods; precocity

He who
would go out of his way not to crush a slug in the mud
crushed her face in the mud
                over a period of
years
because he thought he had some
alternative.
Her puffy face, gazing
with scorn, without hope
into the camera at Ibaraki.

I failed you
and now I am trying to un-fail you

big ragged clouds just
        perceptibly moving south
vast events in their world
        like the tiny spiderlines
from clod-head to clod-head across the ploughed field
in the same sun

So may the soul long animate thy members.
                                      Inf. 16.64-5

tipping my hat to all monuments

looks around furtively before he
        takes his hat off to this oak
with its small plastic plaque:
'Remembered Always'
        (no name):
man gone down to his long home,
with the dismembered bird
and the dried ivy.

bends down to do up his boot
and starts up a pheasant rattling,
a bent rocket

Clouds of leaves
blowing down from the oaks
and crows among them.

a very special red
suffusing the upper branches of this bush:
not my eyes, but
the dying sun behind me
lighting up the whole eye-sweep of
    the woods
between me and the Wolds:

farewell sun, transformer,
where the winds clap-to
stiff leaves against branch
in the empty bush.

In the morning
sky limpid,
pale blue,
grading to rose;
down to the farthest edge
already light;

frost picked out already, white

when the author of it all, a
broad rich-orange band,
slips upward, makes himself known,
and is gone for the day
behind cloud.

striking out for a splash:
to be noticed, accepted

She to me: 'I was in love with you'

There wasn't much to be in love with,
a bubble, a fizz,
a dependence.

'I can't get through to him.' She to Christine

tōmarakago, a basket for transporting criminals.

Ancient instinct
         to cover my tracks:
walking in the line of the wheel-trace
rather than in fresh snow.
Now on the tracks of a moorhen,
broad, simple, elegant,
three-splayed,
who walked this way,
and whose traces I'll cover.

as she faded from my life
I faded

Washed out on Theddlethorpe
sands, while the foam
retreats. A few gulls, a few
sandpipers;
windmills in the distance,
and a faint trail along the sand.

repeating forever the same poem

寂 JAKU death of a priest; quietly.

Abbey Farm leans down to the east,
        the line of the roof-ridge;
always has;
too late to catch the sun lingering, he's got
ways to go,
other worlds to illuminate
there-down.

Small jet-trails, fireflies, streak the sky
in contrary directions
one of them, no doubt, towards that world where
                                        my past lives,

fragments of it,
                the most living (?),
the most missed

A single tree,
        barely to be made out;
a flat horizon, the field edge;
beyond that, nothing.

Is it gone?
All the illusions, gone?
That if I
    huffed and puffed
        (and I did huff and puff)
something would persist

Diary of a tree-stump:
on the third day it rained,
and I did you honour.

On the fourth day, a little sunshine,
and I did you honour.
Everybody believed I did you honour
and it did you no good;
you were elsewhere.

A small bird too small to be a blackbird
flits along *inside* the hedge
keeping out of the wind;

somewhere, up there, the talk of the
　　　hundred and fifteen geese
beating against this sou'-westerly
till they're gone.

OTHER POEMS

Wickenby Aerodrome

At the intersection of the brick circles
             (cracked)   (flaked)
where the one giant swill met the other
(they filtered the condoms)
the sewage of the war effort

and the blood and sweat

washed from the blankets, and the undervests,
             borne in the sanitary napkins

sweat of fear, towards dusk
sweat of fear, over the target,
sweat of fear, jumped

when the instrument readings started to disagree with
what they saw through the clouds

sweat of fear, approaching the runway,
     tired, crusted, blind, and with unknown damage
under the wings

caked, dried, salted and washed
laundered out

to be filtered
     and trickled into the streams
where the bombers made all roar and
shudder as they took off overhead

quietly into the old culverts
      between the hedges
to the beck

where the watervoles resumed their activities

In memoriam M. S.

Gatepost inclined south
across a dry ditch full of leaves
with your heart now occupied by mushrooms,
your grain opened wide, corners edged with moss
and a stout forged hinge-post sticking
out of you,
I'm curious that there should ever have been a gate
here. Why here?

But this would have been in the time of Ivy Lodge
Farm, and the Herd of Pedigree Friesians
and Douglas, and Walter, and Hilary
braves gens
now so long
        (half a lifetime)
                gone
whose daughter, the brave Monica, is now dying

Pale and grey
        shadow of herself,
restless and fretful,
surfacing out of dreams, re-sinking
slipping in and out of dreams and
resurfacing

How to be with you, now

But maybe you are at Ivy Lodge Farm,
                    when we were all young
with the sound of Hilary's voice
with the sun on the beaten earth
                    where it swelled up towards the house
from the barn
          with the one-cylinder Marshall with the flywheel
and the men making jokes
and the smell of the Friesians

Evading

You think you are here
                    invisible:
a headlight shows
on a ground
perfectly even,
        perfectly grey,
and then gone. Branches steadily drip;
Falling mizzle.
One warm window,
        light through a blind in bright fire-orange
from the lonely spinster.

Should I call?
Would it alleviate my guilt
        if I called?
or my loneliness?
How do I know she's lonely?
She wouldn't admit to being lonely,
        and I wouldn't know.
Take refuge in my melancholy and
        the dripping mist
and plod on.

The heritage

Monday 3rd January, 2022,
sun going down over the green,
cutting across the young crops,
blinding the poet.
Park your notebook on top of a barrel,
part of the machinery for breeding up
        pheasants to be shot;
a volley of them shoots off from among the
arrow-like leaves of the dead maize
horizontal in the wind.

And in May:
the wind whistles across the monocultural wheat
with the yard-wide beige border
where the pesticide blocked the invasion
      of the other kinds.
                Ô dandelions
      whose rich orange grades to
bright yellow,
you are an
      other kind.

Old beck dredged out to slack brown
hurrying the degraded soil along to
      the river and sea;
thank you, farmers, if such is the
      name you still go by, for bequeathing us
this

Meditations while sculpting

And God created marble out of small
seashells and let it lie there a few million years
and man dug it up, and converted large
parts of it to white powder in order that
what was left
in the form of shapely
buttocks and eyes with no iris
might magnify his own
soul. The blown dust on the workbench
ripples, and forms
its own furrows and waves, as the laws
that laid down the same marble a few
million years ago still provide.

One corner of a foreign field

What will happen to the leech when it dies
                    with my blood in it? it will shrivel
and be part of the mulch feeding
          the next bamboo: whose new leaves
will be eaten by the deer

between whose toes there will live
          (that's where they like to live)
the next leech,

          until it drops off,
to wait for the blood of the next
human to pass by
                    to feed on,

who will not be me

Consumed

Ô log, dumped on the pile in my stove,
to be eaten away from below
by the heat,
and to pass on, upward,
                    the eating-away
to the logs dumped on after you –
is this life? to be
kicked into motion by some fierce
energy, and mere valencies, and do
nothing, ultimately, but be converted into ash
and pass the same energy
on.
        The ash accumulates
and chokes itself;
the next log's piled in.

Waterdrops

The same halo
I noticed at Ibaraki, 40 years back:
I move, it moves
      round the shadow of my moving head:
light from the bright beads
          on the young kale
around my shadow
from the sun that's now warming my back.

Which then, in that time, at Ibaraki
      must have been the morning sun
on the young rice,
the sheen on the soft blades,
as I biked by the river;
now from melting frost,
long past noon.

Boyhood

Father gets on the train with his
young son, and then gets off again
to go and buy something. How I,
at his age, would have been filled with dread
to be left there alone on the train like that.
And here am I, seul,
seul, seulet; let us
read our newspaper, let us reach for our glasses.
But in fact he is a bit troubled, the boy,
and I with him.

Growing up

They are the ones
whose opinion of me I would like to change
because it affected me so much ... then ...
whose opinion of me will
        never change
because it was formed
then, in my youth,
when I was as transparent as an
        eyeball.
To them, I am now.

Ingram Content Group UK Ltd.
Milton Keynes UK
UKHW011118180423
420361UK00001B/102

9 784907 359423